from SEA TO SHINING SEA

NORTH DAKOTA

By Dennis Brindell Fradin and Judith Bloom Fradin

CONSULTANTS

Ann Rathke, M.A., Historian, State Historical Society of North Dakota

Robert L. Hillerich, Ph.D., Professor Emeritus, Bowling Green State University;
Consultant, Pinellas County Schools, Florida

CHILDRENS PRESS®
CHICAGO

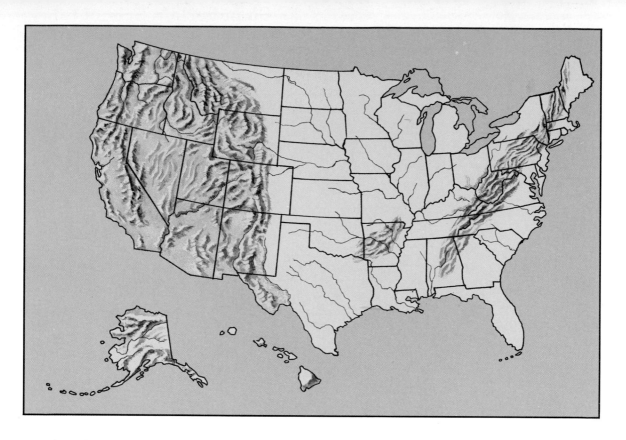

North Dakota is one of the twelve states in the region called the Midwest. The other Midwest states are Illinois, Indiana, Iowa, Kansas, Michigan, Minnesota, Missouri, Nebraska, Ohio, South Dakota, and Wisconsin.

For the wonderful people of North Dakota

Front cover picture: Red River Valley farmland; page 1: Winter in the Badlands; back cover: Cannonball formations, Theodore Roosevelt National Park

Project Editor: Joan Downing
Design Director: Karen Kohn
Typesetting: Graphic Connections, Inc.
Engraving: Liberty Photoengraving

Library of Congress Cataloging-in-Publication Data

Fradin, Dennis B.
  North Dakota / by Dennis Brindell Fradin and Judith Bloom Fradin.
    p.   cm. — (From sea to shining sea)
  Includes index.
  ISBN 0-516-03834-6
  1. North Dakota—Juvenile literature. [1. North Dakota.] I. Fradin, Judith Bloom. II. Title. III. Series: Fradin, Dennis B. From sea to shining sea.
F636.3.F68   1994   94-4871
978.4—dc20   CIP
                                              AC

Table of Contents

Young people taking part in a United Tribes International Powwow in Bismarck

INTRODUCING THE FLICKERTAIL STATE

North Dakota is a big state in the midwestern United States. It was named after the Lakota, or Dakota, Indians. Their name means "friends." The Lakota are also known as the Sioux. Many flickertail ground squirrels live in North Dakota. From them, the state got its main nickname —the Flickertail State.

North Dakota was settled in the late 1800s and early 1900s. The Red River Valley has some of the world's richest farmland. Today, North Dakota ranks second in the country at growing wheat. It is first at growing sunflower seeds and barley.

North Dakota is a great state to live in. It has the country's lowest rate of violent crime. The state's high-school dropout rate is also the country's lowest.

The Flickertail State is special in other ways. What state shares the International Peace Garden with Canada? Where were Eric Sevareid and Peggy

Lee born? Where did baseball slugger Roger Maris grow up? Where are there towns named Zap and Wing? Where did Theodore Roosevelt ranch before he became president? The answer to these questions is: North Dakota!

Overleaf: *A view of Theodore Roosevelt National Park*

A picture map of North Dakota

DUNNINGTON

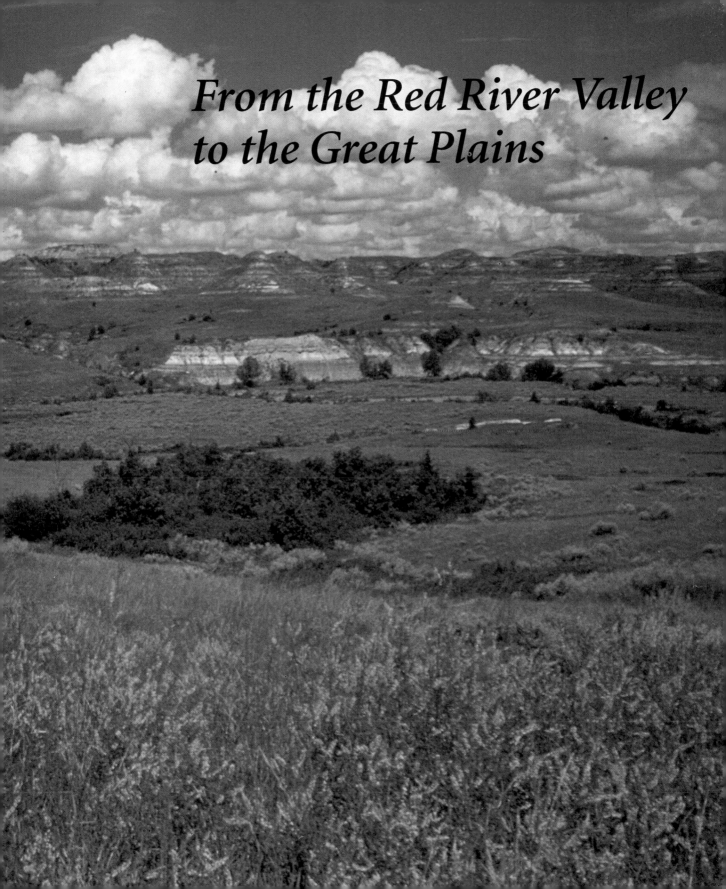

From the Red River Valley
to the Great Plains

FROM THE RED RIVER VALLEY TO THE GREAT PLAINS

Prairie coneflowers in Theodore Roosevelt National Park

North Dakota is in the center of North America. The continent's exact center is near Rugby. North Dakota is also one of the Midwest states. It covers 70,702 square miles. The state is shaped like a rectangle. Three of its borders are straight lines. But the state's eastern border is wavy. It is formed by the Red and the Bois de Sioux rivers. Across these rivers is Minnesota. To the south lies South Dakota. Montana is to the west. Canada lies to the north. Most of North Dakota is covered by flatlands and rolling hills. The Red River Valley is in the east. Large wheat and sugar-beet crops are grown there. Most North Dakotans live in the eastern part of the state. Prairie land is in the middle of the state. It, too, is good for farming. To the north stand the low Pembina and Turtle mountains. The Great Plains begin in western North Dakota. Beef cattle graze there on short prairie grasses. Much oil and coal is found under the ground. In the southwest, buttes rise up sharply above the plains. White Butte is the state's highest point. It stands 3,506 feet above sea level.

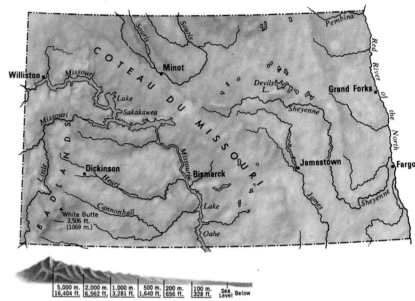

Williston
Missouri
Minot
Souris
Souris
Pembina
COTEAU DU MISSOURI
Lake
Sakakawea
Devils L.
Grand Forks
Sheyenne
Red River of the North
Missouri
BADLANDS
Little
Heart
Dickinson
Bismarck
Missouri
James
Jamestown
Fargo
Cannonball
Lake
Sheyenne
White Butte
3,506 ft.
(1069 m.)
Lake
Oahe

| 5,000 m. 16,404 ft. | 2,000 m. 6,562 ft. | 1,000 m. 3,281 ft. | 500 m. 1,640 ft. | 200 m. 656 ft. | 100 m. 328 ft. | Sea Level | Below |

CLIMATE

Left: Winter, near Northwood

North Dakota is famous for its long, cold winters. The temperature drops to 0 degrees Fahrenheit about fifty-five times each winter. North Dakota's record low was minus 60 degrees Fahrenheit. About 3 feet of snow falls on the state each winter. At times, snowstorms driven by high winds occur there. These are called blizzards.

Huge North Dakota sunflowers

North Dakota also has hot summers. The temperature hits 90 degrees Fahrenheit on about fifteen days. The state's record high was 121 degrees Fahrenheit. North Dakota's rainfall tends to be light. But most of it comes between April and September. That is when farmers need the rain.

9

RIVERS AND LAKES

The Missouri is North Dakota's main river. The "Big Muddy" flows south through the state's western half. North Dakota's Little Missouri, Cannonball, Heart, and Knife rivers flow into the Missouri. The Red River of the North begins at Wahpeton. This river flows northward 545 miles. Its journey ends in Hudson Bay, in Canada. North Dakota's Sheyenne and Maple rivers flow into the Red River. The James is another important North Dakota river.

North Dakota has hundreds of natural lakes. Devils Lake is the largest of them. Lake Sakakawea covers 486 square miles. It was formed by damming the Missouri River. It is the country's largest artificially made lake completely in one state.

Another Red River flows through New Mexico, Texas, Arkansas, and Louisiana.

Left: A cottonwood tree Right: A howling coyote

WOODS AND WILDLIFE

North Dakota is one of the least wooded states. Only one hundredth of the state has forests. Trees grow along the rivers and in some hilly areas. The American elm is the state tree. Ashes, oaks, cottonwoods, and willows grow in North Dakota, too. The wild prairie rose is the state flower.

The western meadowlark is the state bird. Ducks, pheasants, and blue jays also fly about North Dakota. The northern pike is the state fish. Catfish and trout are also found in North Dakota's waters. Flickertail squirrels flick, or jerk, their tails as they run. The state's prairie dogs are also squirrels. Badgers, bobcats, coyotes, white-tailed deer, and pronghorn antelopes live in North Dakota, too.

Wind Canyon and the Little Missouri River, Theodore Roosevelt National Park

Pronghorns are North America's fastest animal. They can run over 60 miles per hour.

11

From Ancient Times Until Today

From Ancient Times Until Today

More than 100 million years ago, dinosaurs roamed across North Dakota. Tyrannosaurus rex stomped about. Triceratops also lived in North Dakota. In 1963, remains of one of these three-horned dinosaurs was found there.

The Ice Age began about 2 million years ago. Glaciers covered most of eastern North Dakota. As these ice sheets moved, they smoothed the land. About 10,000 years ago, the ice melted. The water formed a huge lake. It covered parts of present-day North Dakota, Minnesota, and Canada. Scientists call it Lake Agassiz. Later, this lake drained away. Rich soil was left behind. Today, part of the lake's bed is the Red River Valley.

American Indians

The first North Dakotans were ancient nomadic Indians. They reached North Dakota at least 12,000 years ago. With spears, they hunted giant prehistoric bison. They also hunted elephantlike mammoths and mastodons.

Opposite: Prairie settlers helping a neighbor with his farmwork

Prehistoric Indian picture writing (pictographs) is carved into Writing Rock, near Grenora.

Around A.D. 1000, groups of people were living in villages along the Missouri River. Those groups included Mandan, Hidatsa, and Arikara. They grew corn, sunflowers, beans, and squash. They also hunted buffalo. Their homes were logs covered by dirt. This lifestyle lasted into historic times.

The Sioux, Chippewa, and Assiniboine lived in the northeast. They were mainly hunters. The Cree also lived in North Dakota. Later, the Sioux chased buffalo across the western plains. They ate buffalo meat. They used buffalo skins to make clothing and tepees (tents).

Swiss artist Karl Bodmer painted these portraits of an Assiniboine girl (left) and a Hidatsa chief in 1833.

European Explorers and Fur Traders

In the early 1600s, France set up trading posts in Canada. By 1682, France claimed much of the present-day United States. The French called this land Louisiana. It included all of North Dakota. In 1713, England gained part of Canada, including northeast North Dakota. In 1738, Pierre La Vérendrye, a French Canadian, entered North Dakota. With him were his three sons and a nephew. They were the first known Europeans in North Dakota. The Vérendrye party visited Mandan villages near present-day Bismarck.

France gave Louisiana to Spain in 1762. Spanish traders brought goods up the Missouri River to the Mandans. In exchange, the Spanish received beaver furs. In 1797, David Thompson explored England's North Dakota land. He went down the western Turtle Mountains and along the Souris River. French and English fur traders also came from Canada. They built trading posts and traded for furs with the Indians.

In 1801, Alexander Henry built North Dakota's first permanent trading post. It was part of an English fur-trading company in Canada. Henry's post marked the start of Pembina. This is now

A statue of Pierre La Vérendrye

15

North Dakota's oldest town. Two historic births occurred there. In 1802, a daughter was born to Pierre Bonza and his Indian wife. Bonza was a black man who worked for Henry. The child was North Dakota's first-known partly non-Indian baby. In 1807, North Dakota's first white baby was born. His Scottish parents worked at Henry's post.

AMERICAN EXPLORERS AND SETTLERS

By 1732, England had set up thirteen colonies along the Atlantic Ocean. The colonies declared their independence in 1776. They became the United States of America. By 1783, the United States owned all land east of the Mississippi River. But the new country wanted more land to the west. In 1803, France sold all of Louisiana to the United States. For $15 million, the United States received all French land west of the Mississippi River. This included southwest North Dakota.

President Thomas Jefferson sent Meriwether Lewis and William Clark into the Louisiana Territory. They were to find a route to the Pacific Ocean. They were also to map and describe the land. Lewis and Clark set out from near St. Louis, Missouri, in May 1804. They followed the Missouri

River into central North Dakota. In October, they met friendly Mandan and Hidatsa Indians. They also met Sakakawea, a young Shoshone woman. Years before, she had been kidnapped by the Hidatsa. Lewis and Clark built Fort Mandan. They passed the winter there.

The explorers set out again in April 1805. With them were Sakakawea and her husband, a French-Canadian fur trader. Sakakawea carried their baby on her back. She guided the explorers to the Pacific. She found food for them. Sakakawea also made peace with other Indians they met. In September 1806, the Lewis and Clark party returned to Fort

Her name is also spelled Sacagawea *or* Sacajawea.

Left: A reconstruction of Fort Mandan, near Washburn
Right: A statue of Sakakawea

North Dakota's oldest school was built in Pembina in 1818.

Mandan. Sakakawea remained there. Lewis and Clark continued back to St. Louis.

Lewis and Clark reported that North Dakota had good farmland. But few Americans settled there in the early 1800s. North Dakota's first settlers were Scottish people from Canada. In 1812, these people built a log village at Pembina. But fur traders around Pembina made life difficult for the settlers. Then, in 1818, northeast North Dakota became part of the United States. The people from Canada were then on American land. By 1823, they had all left.

In 1861, the United States Congress created the Dakota Territory. It contained present-day North and South Dakota. Parts of Wyoming and Montana were included, too. On New Year's Day, 1863, the territory was opened to homesteaders. Settlers could receive free land. But they had to live on it and care for it. Still, few people moved to North Dakota. Poor roads, no railroads, and hard winters kept them away. In 1870, North Dakota had only 2,405 people.

In the 1870s, North Dakota finally started to grow. Fargo and Grand Forks were begun in 1871. Bismarck was started in 1872. In that year, North Dakota's first railroad reached Fargo. In 1873, it

stretched to Bismarck. The railroads brought more people and supplies to North Dakota. By 1880, nearly 37,000 people lived in North Dakota. Many came from states to the east. Others came from Norway, Sweden, and Germany.

In forested areas, they built wooden houses. But most of North Dakota was treeless. In such places, settlers cut up chunks of the ground. They piled up these dirt bricks to build sod houses. The "soddies" were warm. In the spring, wildflowers bloomed on their roofs.

In the middle 1870s, many settlers started planting wheat. In the Red River Valley, giant wheat

Sod houses at Rock Lake, about 1906

The wheat was milled into flour or made into cereal and other foods.

19

This constitutional convention parade was held in Bismarck on July 4, 1889.

farms were begun. Their harvests were so great that they were called bonanza farms. About 1878, cattle ranching started in western North Dakota. The railroads carried wheat and cattle to eastern markets.

THE GROWTH OF A GREAT FARMING STATE

In the 1880s, people in the Dakota Territory began seeking statehood. But they wanted two states to be formed. Congress divided the territory into North Dakota and South Dakota. Both Dakotas became states on November 2, 1889.

Which Dakota was made a state first? Not even President Benjamin Harrison knew. He covered the names as he signed the statehood papers. That way neither state could brag about being first. But *n* comes before *s* in the alphabet. So North Dakota became the thirty-ninth state. South Dakota is the fortieth state.

Education was important in North Dakota. The University of North Dakota had opened in 1883. Present-day North Dakota State University started in 1890. North Dakota's first public library opened at Grafton in 1897. By 1900, the young state had 319,146 people.

North Dakota has twenty colleges. That is a lot for a state with so few people.

In the early 1900s, many North Dakota farmers were angry. Banks, railroads, and flour mills were making money. The farmers wanted their fair share. In 1915, the Nonpartisan League (NPL) was formed in North Dakota. It worked on behalf of the state's farmers. Within a year, the NPL had 30,000 members. In 1916, the NPL helped elect Lynn Frazier as governor. He was a teacher and farmer. Frazier had grown up in a North Dakota sod house.

Governor Frazier and the NPL made many changes in North Dakota. The Bank of North Dakota was begun at Bismarck in 1919. This was a state-owned bank. It gave low-interest loans to

The state-owned Bank of North Dakota

North Dakota farmers and businesses. The state-owned North Dakota Mill and Elevator opened at Grand Forks in 1922. It helped wheat farmers obtain better prices. The state government also lowered certain farm taxes. More money was spent on rural schools.

Meanwhile, World War I (1914-1918) was being fought in Europe. At first, the United States stayed out of the war. North Dakotans agreed with this. In 1915, North Dakota's governor, Louis B. Hanna, sailed to Europe. Other American leaders went also. This group tried to persuade European leaders to end the war. They failed to do so.

Left: The North Dakota Mill and Elevator, at Grand Forks
Right: Farmers seeding fields in the 1880s

The United States finally entered World War I in 1917. Many North Dakotans still opposed the war. Yet, nearly 30,000 North Dakota soldiers helped win it. North Dakota wheat was made into food for American troops.

In the 1920s, other crops besides wheat gained importance. North Dakota became the country's top barley grower in 1925. Today, it still ranks first. Sugar beets and red potatoes also became important. The growing of new crops attracted new people. By 1930, the Flickertail State was home to 680,845 people.

THE GREAT DEPRESSION AND WORLD WAR II

The Great Depression hit the country in 1929. Until 1939, Americans went through hard times. The stock market crashed. Banks closed around the country. Farm prices fell. In North Dakota, drought struck in 1929. The dry period continued into the 1930s. Each year between 1931 and 1936, North Dakota suffered from dust storms. North Dakotans called these years the "Dirty Thirties."

The depression may have hurt North Dakota more than any other state. By 1933, North Dakotans were earning one-third the income of

These sand dunes were formed near Granville during the droughts of the 1930s.

other Americans. By 1936, about one-half of North Dakotans were receiving government aid. By 1939, one-third of the state's farmers had lost their land. Many of them moved to other states. Between 1930 and 1940, North Dakota lost almost 39,000 people.

North Dakotans learned from the dry years of the 1930s. In 1937, the state created the North Dakota Water Conservation Commission. Soon, all fifty-three of the state's counties had started water projects. Ways to save water and protect the soil were studied.

In 1941, the United States entered World War II (1939-1945). Again, many North Dakotans opposed the war. Yet, again, North Dakota did its share once the country declared war. About 70,000 of the state's men and women served. North Dakota's farmers supplied large amounts of food for the troops.

MODERN TIMES

After World War II, many changes came to North Dakota. As farmers used more machinery, farm workers lost their jobs. Many moved to North Dakota's towns and cities. In the 1950s, North Dakotans became more closely linked to other

Americans. Present-day KXMC-TV began broadcasting in Minot. It was North Dakota's first television station. North Dakota's interstate highways were begun in 1956. Airline service to and within North Dakota also grew in the 1950s.

Garrison Dam was completed on the Missouri River in 1960. It is one of the world's biggest earthen dams. The dam created Lake Sakakawea. The lake provides water for crops. Water at the dam generates electricity for thousands of North Dakotans. In 1968, the Garrison Diversion Project started. It will bring huge amounts of Missouri River water to cities and farms. Some say the project will be too costly, however. They also claim it will cause pollu-

Garrison Dam

An oil rig in Burke County

tion and harm wildlife. How to continue it is still an issue in North Dakota.

In 1951, oil was found near Tioga. Oil refineries opened at Williston and Mandan. In 1978, a huge oil boom began in western North Dakota. Thousands of oil workers poured into the state. In Williston, many of them slept in tents until homes were built. By 1984, North Dakota was producing 53 million barrels of oil a year. The state had become a leading oil producer.

Oil prices fell in 1986, however. North Dakota's oil production fell with it. Thousands of people left Williston and other oil towns. Some who remained could not pay their taxes. They lost their homes.

Meanwhile, North Dakota's farmers were having hard times again. Prices for land, machinery, and seed rose. Prices paid for crops and cattle did not keep pace. Blizzards and floods destroyed animals and fields in the 1970s. Heat and drought did the same in the 1980s. There were 45,000 farms and ranches in North Dakota in 1970. That number had fallen to 33,000 by 1993. The farmers' troubles hurt other businesses. For example, sales of farm machinery fell. Clothing and hardware stores closed. Between 1980 and 1990, North Dakota lost more than 11,000 people.

The Flickertail State turned 100 years old in 1989. North Dakotans celebrated in many ways. They held Native American Day to honor North Dakota's Indians. Lewis and Clark's trip was recreated. People dressed as pioneers.

Long ago, pioneers had come to North Dakota looking for a better life. Today's North Dakotans also have reasons to be hopeful. They live in a state where the air and water are clean. The people are friendly. In the early 1990s, North Dakota gained 25,000 new jobs. Trade with Canada and Mexico is growing. Tourism is increasing as well. North Dakotans expect these good times to continue past the year 2000.

Thousands of people enjoyed North Dakota's centennial celebration in the summer of 1989.

Overleaf: A young girl on a trail ride in Theodore Roosevelt National Park

North Dakotans and Their Work

North Dakotans and Their Work

The 1990 Census counted exactly 638,800 North Dakotans. Only Wyoming, Alaska, and Vermont have fewer people. The state averages just nine people per square mile.

Of every 100 North Dakotans, 95 are white. Nearly one-half of the state's people are of German background. More than one-fifth trace their roots to Norway. Many others had families who came from England, Ireland, or Sweden.

North Dakota is home to about 26,000 American Indians. Many live on North Dakota's four Indian reservations. Others make their homes in cities or towns. There are about 12,000 Chippewa. That is North Dakota's largest Indian group. The Sioux, with 7,000 people, come next.

Nearly 5,000 North Dakotans are Hispanic. North Dakota has 3,500 black people. The state is also home to 3,500 people of Asian background.

How They Are Special

North Dakota is one of the safest states. Its murder rate is the country's lowest. So is its robbery rate. A

Most people who live in North Dakota are white, but the state is also home to about 26,000 American Indians.

Rodeo Days, in Mandan

safe life helps North Dakotans live about seventy-six years.

North Dakotans prize education. Only 4 out of 10 students drop out of high school. That is the lowest rate in the country. North Dakota also spends much money on its colleges. They get a higher rate of tax money than colleges in other states.

EARNING A LIVING IN NORTH DAKOTA

Almost 300,000 North Dakotans have jobs. Close to 70,000 workers sell goods. Many work in grocery and hardware stores. Others sell such items as cars and farm equipment.

About 66,000 of the state's workers provide services. They include lawyers, doctors, and nurses. Car and tractor repairers are counted, too. Service workers are important in North Dakota. Often, North Dakotans must drive more than 50 miles to find a gas station or a doctor.

Another 66,000 North Dakotans have government jobs. They include teachers and workers on Indian reservations. They also include people on military bases. Large air force bases are at Grand Forks and Minot.

Minot Air Force Base

Nearly 40,000 North Dakotans farm or ranch. Wheat is their main product. North Dakota trails only Kansas at growing wheat. The Flickertail State leads the country at growing sunflower seeds and barley. Flaxseed is another leading crop. The state is second in the country at growing dry beans. It is among the top four growers of oats, sugar beets, potatoes, and rye.

North Dakota has almost 2 million head of cattle. Some of them provide milk. Most are beef cattle. Many sheep and hogs are also raised in North Dakota. Some farmers keep bees. They make 20 million pounds of honey each year.

A farmer harvesting wheat near Bismarck

More than 16,000 North Dakotans make products. Packaged foods lead the list. Bread, meat, and sugar are among these foods. Other North Dakota products include farm machines, buses, and airplane parts.

Mining employs about 4,000 North Dakotans. Oil is the top mining product. Lignite coal and natural gas are two other North Dakota fuels. The state has one of the world's largest lignite deposits. This lignite is burned to provide electricity for North Dakota and nearby states.

A North Dakota lignite coal mine

Overleaf: The state capitol, in Bismarck

33

A North Dakota Tour

A North Dakota Tour

North Dakota has many interesting places to visit. The Flickertail State is known for its many pioneer sites. The state also has Indian reservations and a national park. Blue lakes and fields of golden wheat add to the state's beauty.

The Southeast

Fargo is on the state's far eastern edge. It lies on the Red River. Fargo was begun in 1871. It was named for William Fargo. He was a founder of the Wells, Fargo Express Company. Today, Fargo is North Dakota's largest city. More than 74,000 people live there. North Dakota State University (NDSU) is at Fargo. NDSU is a leader at improving crops. New kinds of sunflowers and wheat have been started there.

Bonanzaville, USA, is nearby at West Fargo. This is a pioneer village. It was named for the bonanza farms. Visitors can tour more than forty buildings. They include log cabins, sod houses, a schoolhouse, and a jail.

The Cass County District Court House in Bonanzaville, USA

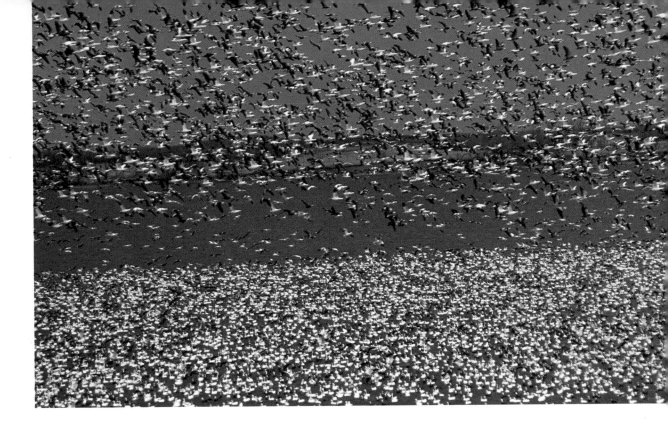

To the south is Fort Abercrombie. This was North Dakota's first permanent United States military post. It was built in 1857. The fort withstood a six-week attack by the Sioux in 1862. Nearby is Bagg Bonanza Farm. It is North Dakota's last complete bonanza farm. The farm is being restored to look as it did in the early 1900s.

In far southeastern North Dakota is Tewaukon National Wildlife Refuge. Ducks, geese, and herons can be seen there. Chase Lake National Wildlife Refuge is to the northwest. It is North America's largest breeding ground for white pelicans. Each spring, about 15,000 pelicans can be seen there.

Geese at Tewaukon National Wildlife Refuge

The United States has about 500 national wildlife refuges. Sixty-three of them are in North Dakota. No other state has as many.

This huge buffalo statue is in Frontier Village, at Jamestown. Millions of buffalo once roamed the plains. By 1890, most of them had been killed. Since then, buffalo herds have been re-established in some places.

Jamestown is east of Chase Lake. This city of over 15,000 people is home to Frontier Village. It has many pioneer homes and shops. The world's largest buffalo stands at Frontier Village. Made of concrete and steel, it is 26 feet tall. Jamestown is also home to the National Buffalo Museum. There, visitors can learn about these 1,500-pound animals. A herd of more than twenty buffalo lives in the museum's pasture.

SOUTHWEST

West of Jamestown is Bismarck. This Missouri River city was begun in 1872. It was named for Otto von Bismarck. He was a leader in Germany. North Dakotans hoped to receive money from Germany. They planned to use the money to build more railroads across the state.

Today, nearly 50,000 people live in Bismarck. It is North Dakota's third-biggest city and the state capital. The capitol building is nineteen stories high. It is called the "Skyscraper of the Prairies." In it are paintings of the Theodore Roosevelt Rough Rider Award winners. Each year since 1961, great North Dakotans have received this award. Outside the capitol is a statue of Sakakawea.

The North Dakota Heritage Center is also on the capitol grounds. Displays on the state's history can be seen there. Children enjoy the center's mastodon skeleton. Visitors can view exhibits on the many people who built North Dakota.

Bismarck hosts the United Tribes Powwow each spring and fall. This gathering attracts Indians of many tribes. They come from around the United States and Canada. The public is also invited. Traditional dancing and singing are part of the pow-wow. Indian foods are offered, too. Corn soup and wild rice soup are some favorites.

Across the Missouri River from Bismarck is Mandan. Fort Abraham Lincoln State Park is near-by. George Custer commanded Fort Lincoln until 1876. In that year, he died at the Battle of the Little Bighorn. That was in Montana. Custer's home has been rebuilt at Fort Abraham Lincoln State Park. Visitors can also see a rebuilt Mandan Indian village.

Dickinson is west of Mandan. With more than 16,000 people, Dickinson is the state's fifth-biggest city. The Dakota Dinosaur Museum opened there in 1994. This museum has dinosaur models and bones.

North Dakota's Badlands lie west of Dickinson. The Little Missouri River cuts through this area.

George Armstrong Custer's desk can be seen at Fort Lincoln, near Mandan.

Theodore Roosevelt was born in New York.

Theodore Roosevelt National Park is in the Badlands (below).

Buttes and many strangely shaped formations rise above the land. Water and wind carved the unusual scenery. Theodore Roosevelt National Park is in the Badlands. Roosevelt lived in the Badlands from 1883 to 1886. He owned two cattle ranches there. Roosevelt tended cattle on horseback. Later, he became president of the United States (1901-1909). "I would never have been president if it had not been for my experience in North Dakota," Roosevelt wrote. Today, Roosevelt's cabin can still be seen at the park. The park is also home to buffalo, porcupines, wild horses, and prairie dogs.

Near the south entrance to Theodore Roosevelt National Park is Medora. The Marquis de Mores, a Frenchman, founded this town in 1883. He named it for his wife. The marquis hoped to make Medora a meat-packing center. This didn't happen. But his twenty-six-room home still stands near the town. The house is called Chateau de Mores.

NORTHWEST

Lake Sakakawea lies in northwestern North Dakota. This lake was named for Lewis and Clark's Indian guide. People fish, swim, and water-ski on the lake. Four Bears Bridge spans the lake. The bridge honors Mandan and Hidatsa chiefs. They shared the name Four Bears.

Sailboats on Lake Sakakawea

Lake Sakakawea cuts through Fort Berthold Indian Reservation. It is the largest reservation completely within North Dakota. Mandan, Arikara, and Hidatsa Indians live there. On the reservation is the Three Tribes Museum. It is a good place to learn about these Indians.

Williston is northwest of the Indian reservation. Today, the Williston region produces oil. Long ago, it was known for fur trading. Fort Union is southwest of Williston. It was built in 1829 as a trading

Fort Union Trading Post

post. Today, visitors tour the rebuilt fort. They can see how fur traders once lived and worked. Each year, the fur traders held a big get-together. They called it the rendezvous. Each summer, the fort now hosts the Fort Union Trading Post Rendezvous. Many contests are held, including tomahawk and frying-pan throwing. Fort Buford State Historic Site is southwest of Fort Union. Sitting Bull surrendered to the United States Army there in 1881. He was a great Sioux leader.

In the state's far northwest corner is Writing Rock Historic Site. Prehistoric Indians carved pictures into this huge rock. Many Indians believe this picture writing is holy.

Southeast of Writing Rock is Minot. It lies on the Souris River. Minot was named for Henry Minot, a friend of Theodore Roosevelt. The town was begun in 1886 as the railroad came through. Minot grew rapidly. It became known as the "Magic City." Today, Minot is North Dakota's fourth-biggest city. About 35,000 people live there.

Minot's Roosevelt Park Zoo has giraffes, tigers, and monkeys. The Magic City Express can be boarded near the zoo. This small train takes people through Roosevelt Park. The park has a swimming pool and water slide. Each July, Minot hosts the North Dakota State Fair. The fair offers livestock and crop exhibits. There are stage shows, a rodeo, and food, too. About 300,000 people attend. That is about one-half of the state's population!

A building at Minot's Roosevelt Park Zoo

NORTHEAST

The center of North America is about 70 miles east of Minot. A stone tower at Rugby marks the spot. The Geographical Center Museum is near the tower. There, visitors can learn how the continent's center was determined. North of Rugby is the International Peace Garden. Part of it is in North Dakota. Part is in Canada. The garden honors the friendship between Canada and the United States.

To the east is Walhalla. The Antoine Gingras house and trading post there dates from 1843. It is North Dakota's oldest known building. East of Walhalla is Pembina. It is in the state's far northeast corner. Pembina is North Dakota's oldest non-Indian town. The state's oldest frame schoolhouse is there. North America's largest maker of buses has a plant in Pembina. Millions of people have ridden on Motor Coach Industries' buses.

Grafton is south of Pembina. Close to downtown Grafton is Heritage Village. Visitors can tour a pioneer farmhouse, a country church, and a railroad depot. A working merry-go-round is also in the village.

Farther south is Grand Forks. Nearly 50,000 people live there. That makes it the state's second-biggest city. The University of North Dakota (UND) is at Grand Forks. With 12,000 students, UND is the state's largest school. This college has become known for aerospace science. Many jet pilots have been trained there. The North Dakota

Museum of Art is also at UND. People go there to see modern artworks.

Grand Forks lies at the fork of the Red and Red Lake rivers. Many visitors board the *Dakota Queen* riverboat. They can enjoy an afternoon or evening ride on the Red River. This is a perfect way to end a tour of North Dakota.

The International Peace Garden

A Gallery
of Famous
North
Dakotans

A Gallery of Famous North Dakotans

Many North Dakotans have made their mark on the world. They include an explorer, authors, and a home-run king. **Vilhjalmur Stefansson** (1879-1962) grew up in Mountain. He became an Arctic explorer. Stefansson mapped the land around the North Pole. He discovered several islands. He spent many years living with the Eskimos. Much of what is known about the Arctic is due to Stefansson. His books include *My Life with the Eskimos* and *The Friendly Arctic.*

A stone memorial sits near the courthouse in Center. It honors fifteen-year-old **Hazel Miner** (1904-1920). One afternoon Hazel and her younger brother and sister were returning home from school. A blizzard was raging. Their horse-drawn sled overturned. Hazel covered the two children with a robe. She lay upon it to keep them warm. The three of them were found the next day. Hazel's brother and sister were frostbitten but alive. Hazel had frozen to death saving them.

Brynhild Haugland was born in 1905 near Minot. Her parents had a dairy farm. They often

Opposite: In 1953, a young Roger Maris was a member of the Fargo-Moorhead Twins.

Vilhjalmur Stefansson

Brynhild Haugland (above) won twenty-six straight elections for her house seat.

Eric Sevareid

took her to political meetings. In 1938, Haugland was elected to the North Dakota House of Representatives. There, she worked for studies on better ways of farming. Haugland retired in 1990 after fifty-two years of service.

Era Bell Thompson (1906-1986) was born in Iowa. Her family then moved to North Dakota. Thompson lived in Driscoll and Bismarck. Hers was one of a few black families in North Dakota. While in high school, Thompson wrote for the *Chicago Defender*. Thompson pretended to be "Dakota Dick" from the "wild and wooly West." Later, she became an editor for *Negro Digest* and *Ebony* magazines. Thompson also wrote *American Daughter* and *Africa, Land of My Fathers*. She received a Rough Rider Award in 1976.

Eric Sevareid (1912-1992) was born in Velva. When he was seventeen, he went on a 2,200-mile canoe trip. Sevareid wrote newspaper stories and a children's book about it. Later, he became a famous television broadcaster. Many people remember his thoughtful news reports.

Anne H. Carlsen was born in Wisconsin in 1915. She was born without hands or feet. Her family and friends pulled her around in a wagon. Carlsen wanted to make her own way in the world.

She attended regular schools. Carlsen even earned a doctorate. She became the head of the Crippled Children's School at Jamestown. There, Carlsen taught handicapped children for forty-two years. The school is now called the Anne Carlsen Center for Children.

Lawrence Welk (1903-1992) was born in Strasburg. He grew up in a sod farmhouse. His father taught him to play the accordion. By the age of thirteen, Welk was playing at weddings. He became a famous bandleader. People loved his bubbly dance music. It was called "champagne music." Welk and his band appeared on radio and television.

Era Bell Thompson (center) set five state track records at the University of North Dakota. She was only 4 feet 8 inches tall.

Lawrence Welk and his orchestra with the Lennon Sisters

Angie Dickinson

He had the longest-running musical show in television history (1955-1982).

Peggy Lee was born in Jamestown in 1920. She sang in church and school choirs. Later, she became a singer in a jazz band. Lee is known for her soft, cool singing voice. Between 1945 and 1964, her records outsold those of all other women singers. Lee also wrote songs. Some were used in the movie *Lady and the Tramp.* Lee also was the voice for Peg, the fancy poodle, in that film.

Angie Dickinson was born in Kulm in 1932. After attending college, she won a beauty contest. Her prize was a spot as a dancer on a television show. Dickinson became a movie star. Her movies include *Rio Bravo* and *Cast a Giant Shadow*. In 1974, the television show "Police Woman" was written for her. She played Pepper Anderson, an undercover officer.

Although born in Minnesota, **Roger Maris** (1934-1985) grew up in Fargo. Maris was a football star at Shanley High. But he was even better at baseball. In 1960, he joined the New York Yankees. In 1961, Maris hit sixty-one home runs. That broke Babe Ruth's record of sixty home runs in one year. Maris also won the American League's Most Valuable Player Award (1960-1961). The Roger Maris Museum in Fargo honors him. His New York Yankees uniform and other belongings are shown there.

Phyllis Frelich was born in Devils Lake in 1944. She was the oldest of nine deaf children of deaf parents. Frelich attended the local school for the deaf. Later, she became an actress. In 1980, she starred in *Children of a Lesser God*. This play is about a deaf woman and her hearing husband. Frelich's performance won the 1980 Tony Award for best actress. Frelich also helped found the National Theatre of the Deaf.

Fritz Scholder was born in Minnesota in 1937. He lived in Wahpeton. Scholder won his first art

Peggy Lee

Larry Woiwode (above) won North Dakota's 1992 Rough Rider Award.

prize in fourth grade. When he was in junior high school, he sold his first painting. Scholder won fame for his paintings, prints, and sculpture. Since 1967, most of his works have had Indian themes. Scholder is one-fourth American Indian. He believes in the power of love, art, and magic.

Several outstanding writers have come from North Dakota. **Louis L'Amour** (1908-1988) was born in Jamestown. As a boy, he heard family stories about his pioneer ancestors. L'Amour became a famous writer of Westerns. *Hondo* and *How the West Was Won* are two of his novels. They became movies. Altogether, L'Amour wrote more than 100 books. They have sold 200 million copies in twenty languages.

Larry Woiwode was born in Carrington in 1941. He spent his childhood in nearby Sykeston. In the 1960s, Woiwode began selling stories to major magazines. His first novel was *What I'm Going to Do, I Think* (1969). Many of his works, including *Beyond the Bedroom Wall,* are set in North Dakota.

Louise Erdrich was born in Minnesota in 1954. She grew up in Wahpeton. Erdrich is one-half Chippewa. Her father was a teacher. He encouraged Erdrich to write. When she was small, her father paid her a nickel for every story she wrote. Erdrich

Louis L'Amour, who was born in Jamestown, became a famous writer of Westerns.

has written many short stories and novels. Two of her books are *Love Medicine* and *The Beet Queen*. They tell about North Dakota Chippewa families.

Birthplace of Brynhild Haugland, Louis L'Amour, Lawrence Welk, and Peggy Lee . . .

Home to Vilhjalmur Stefansson, Louise Erdrich, Roger Maris, and Era Bell Thompson . . .

A leading state at growing wheat, barley, and sunflower seeds . . .

The state with the fewest crimes and some of the best schools . . .

This is North Dakota—the Flickertail State!

Did You Know?

A town in the southwest part of the state was named for a little girl. Her name was Margaret Martha. But the town was named for her way of saying her name— Marmarth.

North Dakota has towns named Buffalo, Cannon Ball, Wing, and Zeeland. But, surely, Zap must be given the prize for the North Dakota town with the strangest name.

The breakfast cereal Cream of Wheat was developed at Grand Forks in 1893.

North Dakota had the first woman speaker of a state house of representatives. Minnie Craig held that office from January 3 to March 3, 1933.

The whooping crane, one of North America's rarest birds, can sometimes be seen in North Dakota.

Curling is a popular sport in North Dakota. It involves sliding stones across the ice toward a target. This game started in Europe in the 1600s.

North Dakota State University's women's basketball team won the 1993 Division II championship.

North Dakota's high (121° F.) and low (-60° F.) temperatures both occurred in 1936. That 181 degree temperature difference in one state in one year set a U.S. record.

The KTHI-TV tower near Blanchard is the world's tallest structure. The 2,063-foot tower is 600 feet higher than the Sears Tower in Chicago, which is the world's tallest building.

There was a drive in the 1980s to drop "North" from the state's name. People claimed it made the state sound cold. But, in 1989, state lawmakers refused a request to put the issue to the voters.

In North Dakota and other northern areas, halos of light sometimes appear near the sun. They are called "sun dogs."

North Dakota is the only state to share a golf course with another country. Part of the course is in Portal, North Dakota. The other part is in Saskatchewan, a province in Canada.

The Centennial Trees Program was part of North Dakota's 100th birthday celebration in 1989. The program's goal is to plant 100 million trees by the year 2000.

During dry winters, North Dakotans sometimes say they have *snirt*. This is a mixture of light *snow* and *dirt* that is blown around by the wind.

The Great Northern soup bean was first marketed by a North Dakotan. Bismarck seedman Oscar Will had obtained the bean from an Indian.

NORTH DAKOTA INFORMATION

State flag

Wild prairie rose

Western meadowlark

Area: 70,702 square miles (the seventeenth-biggest state)

Greatest Distance North to South: 210 miles

Greatest Distance East to West: 360 miles

Borders: Canada to the north; Minnesota to the east; Montana to the west; South Dakota to the south

Highest Point: White Butte, 3,506 feet above sea level

Lowest Point: 750 feet above sea level, along the Red River in Pembina County

Hottest Recorded Temperature: 121° F. (at Steele, on July 6, 1936)

Coldest Recorded Temperature: -60° F. (at Parshall, on February 15, 1936)

Statehood: The thirty-ninth state, on November 2, 1889

Origin of Name: North Dakota was named for the Dakota Indians; the word Dakota means "friends" in the Sioux language

Capital: Bismarck

Counties: 53

United States Representatives: 1

State Senators: 53

State Representatives: 106

State Song: "North Dakota Hymn," by James W. Foley (words) and Dr. C. S. Putnam (music)

State Motto: Liberty and Union, Now and Forever, One and Inseparable

Main Nickname: "Flickertail State"

Other Nicknames: "Peace Garden State," "Sioux State," "Rough Rider State," "Friendly State," "Golden Grain State," "Land of the Fresh Horizons"

State Seal: Adopted in 1889

State Flag: Adopted in 1911

State Flower: Wild prairie rose

State Bird: Western meadowlark

State Tree: American elm

State Fish: Northern pike

State Grass: Western wheat grass

State Fossil: Teredo petrified wood

State Beverage: Milk

Rivers: Missouri, Red, Little Missouri, Cannonball, Heart, Knife, James, Sheyenne, Maple, Souris

Lakes: Sakakawea, Devils, Patterson, Bowman-Haley

Wildlife: Western meadowlarks, blue jays, orioles, ducks, geese, pheasants, grouse, great blue herons, whooping cranes, pelicans, many other kinds of birds, northern pike, perch, catfish, coho salmon, chinook salmon, many other kinds of fish, flickertail squirrels, prairie dogs, badgers, bobcats, coyotes, white-tailed deer, pronghorn antelopes, foxes, skunks, beavers, muskrats, mink, buffalo, wild horses, rabbits, porcupines

Manufactured Products: Bread, meat, sugar, other foods, farm machines, buses, airplane parts, bricks, newspapers

Farm Products: Wheat, sunflower seeds, barley, flaxseed, dry beans, oats, sugar beets, potatoes, rye, honey, beef cattle, milk, sheep, hogs

Mining Products: Oil, coal, natural gas, sand and gravel

Population: 638,800, forty-seventh among the states (1990 U.S. Census Bureau figures)

American elm trees

Prairie dog

Major Cities (1990 Census):

Fargo	74,111	Jamestown	15,571
Grand Forks	49,425	Mandan	15,177
Bismarck	49,256	Williston	13,131
Minot	34,544	West Fargo	12,287
Dickinson	16,097	Wahpeton	8,751

North Dakota History

Members of a pioneer family pose in front of their tar-paper shack at Rock Lake.

10,000 B.C.—The first people reach North Dakota

1682—France claims a large area of North America, including part of what is now North Dakota

1713—England receives the northern part of North Dakota from France

1738—French explorer Pierre Vérendrye becomes the first-known European explorer to enter North Dakota

1776—The United States of America is created

1801—Alexander Henry builds North Dakota's first permanent trading post at Pembina

1803—The United States obtains southwestern North Dakota from France in the Louisiana Purchase

1804-06—The Lewis and Clark Expedition is helped by Sakakawea, a North Dakota Indian woman

1812—People from Canada attempt to build a town at Pembina

1818—The United States gains control of the rest of North Dakota through a treaty with England

1857—Fort Abercrombie, North Dakota's first U.S. military post, is established

1861—The U.S. Congress creates the Dakota Territory

1863—The Dakota Territory is opened to homesteaders

1864—The *Frontier Scout,* North Dakota's first newspaper, is issued at Fort Union

1871—Fargo and Grand Forks are begun

1872—Bismarck is founded; the first railroad arrives in North Dakota

1873—The *Bismarck Tribune,* now the state's oldest newspaper still in print, begins publication

1875—Bonanza wheat farms begin in the Red River Valley

1878—Ranching begins in western North Dakota